SPOTLIGHT ON GLOBAL ISSUES

FEEDING A CHANGING PLANET

Amanda Vink

ROSEN PUBLISHING
NEW YORK

Published in 2022 by The Rosen Publishing Group, Inc.
29 East 21st Street, New York, NY 10010

First Edition

Editor: Theresa Emminizer
Book Design: Michael Flynn

Photo Credits: Cover Jukov studio/Shutterstock.com; (series globe background) photastic/Shutterstock.com; p. 04 Monkey Business Images/Shutterstock.com; p. 5 nito/Shutterstock.com; p. 7 (Upton Sinclair) Buyenlarge/Archive Photos/Getty Images; p. 7 (book) Bettmann/Getty Images; p. 8 iliuta goean/Shutterstock.com; p. 9 selimaksan/iStock/Getty Images; p. 10 WIN-Initiative/Stone/Getty Images; p. 11 The Washington Post/Getty Images; p. 12 symbiot/Shutterstock.com; p. 13 Gestalt Imagery/Shutterstock.com; p. 14 PixieMe/Shutterstock.com; p. 15 (alfalfa sprouts) Ildi Papp/Shutterstock.com; p. 15 (lentils) monticello/Shutterstock.com; p. 16 El Nariz/Shutterstock.com; p. 17 courtesy of choosemyplate.gov; p. 18 Antonina Vlasova/Shutterstock.com; p. 19 Rawpixel.com/Shutterstock.com; p. 21 Rawpixel/iStock/Getty Images; p. 22 fstop123/iStock/Getty Images; p. 23 mythja/Shutterstock.com; p. 25 Niall Carson/PA Images/Getty Images; p. 27 Sundry Photography/Shutterstock.com; p. 28 Africa Studio/Shutterstock.com; p. 29 https://commons.wikimedia.org/wiki/File:Obama_signs_FSMA_into_Law.jpg; p. 30 kryzhov/Shutterstock.com.

Library of Congress Cataloging-in-Publication Data

Names: Vink, Amanda, author.
Title: Feeding a changing planet / Amanda Vink.
Description: New York : PowerKids Press, [2022] | Series: Spotlight on global issues | Includes index.
Identifiers: LCCN 2020000886 | ISBN 9781725323391 (paperback) | ISBN 9781725323421 (library binding) | ISBN 9781725323407 (6 pack)
Subjects: LCSH: Food supply--Juvenile literature. | Food security--Juvenile literature.
Classification: LCC HD9000.5 .V56 2022 | DDC 338.1/9--dc23
LC record available at https://lccn.loc.gov/2020000886

Manufactured in the United States of America

CPSIA Compliance Information: Batch #CSR22. For further information contact Rosen Publishing, New York, New York at 1-800-237-9932.

CONTENTS

CHAPTER ONE

ONE MEAL AT A TIME

Some people think that as individuals, we're too small to make much of a difference in the world—but that's not true. If you want to change the world for the better, your diet is a great place to start. That's because a lot of resources go into creating and moving food.

Every living creature on Earth must consume food in order to create enough energy to live. This is part of life, and it's not something to feel guilty about. It is, however, important to take responsibility for yourself and your actions. That means being aware of what you eat and where that food comes from. It also means recognizing that if you have enough to eat each day, you are extremely fortunate.

Currently there's enough food created to feed everyone on the planet, but as the population continues to increase, someday there won't be enough. It's important to take steps now.

On average, a moderately active adult needs between 2,000 and 2,500 calories a day. In some places, not everyone has enough. When a person doesn't know where their next meal is coming from, that's called food insecurity. Today there are more than 821 million people in the world who are regularly underfed.

One of the biggest problems of our time is food distribution. There's more than enough food produced to feed everyone on the planet. In fact, there's more than 1½ times enough, but not everyone has access to this food. This is called food scarcity. In addition, a lot of food in the world is wasted. Roughly a third of the food produced every year, about 1.3 billion tons (1.2 billion mt), is thrown away.

CHAPTER TWO

THE FOOD INDUSTRY

Making sure that everyone has enough to eat is one of the most basic challenges of a society. Civilizations throughout time have developed methods to improve growing and harvesting food. Scientists believe the first agriculture happened in the Fertile Crescent, an area near modern-day Iraq and Syria. This allowed for the rise of cities.

As new technologies developed, new food-processing methods were put into use. The Industrial Revolution had a huge impact on food production. Steamships and refrigeration in the 19th century allowed more food to be shipped internationally. Between the 1850s and 1914, world food exports expanded from 4 million tons (3.6 million mt) to 40 million tons (36.3 million mt). After refrigerated railcars were invented, Chicago became the center for meatpacking in the United States.

Conditions in food-packing plants were not always clean or safe. In 1906, Upton Sinclair published a novel called *The Jungle*, which exposed problems in the meatpacking industry. The novel showed the extremely harsh and dirty conditions workers were forced to endure. Readers were outraged, especially by the unsanitary practices. In 1906, President Theodore Roosevelt signed two bills into law that regulated the food and drug industries.

Today, safety regulations are a very important part of the food industry. Both state and federal agencies provide overviews to make sure that food products meet a certain standard. These regulations include processing and handling of food. For example, in New York State, ready-to-eat food must be prepared and served without coming into contact with bare hands.

After Sinclair's book *The Jungle* was released, the White House began receiving letters calling for food industry reforms.

CHAPTER THREE

FOOD DISTRIBUTION

Industrialized agriculture in the United States and around the world is, at this moment, an unsustainable practice. That means what we're doing right now can't last forever. Many food-growing practices are harmful to the planet. In part because of large-scale industrial agriculture, a third of Earth's soil is degraded. That means it's lost its nutrients and the ability to produce healthful food. In fact, if things continue as they are, the world's topsoil could be gone within 60 years, according to the United Nations (UN). Topsoil is needed for farming.

DEGRADED SOIL IN DANUBE DELTA, ROMANIA

Worldwide hunger doesn't have to be a reality. With the right tools, we can change the situation.

Unless things change, at some point there won't be enough food to support the population of the planet. Even right now, there are too many people all over the world who go hungry. Most hungry people live in low-income countries. Research from the Gallup World Poll in 2017 revealed that 55 percent of people in sub-Saharan Africa have food insecurity, while 28 percent have severe food insecurity. But hunger also affects people in economically secure countries as well.

Having access to safe and healthy food is a fundamental human right. The sad fact is that many people don't have access to food because of power imbalances. Some people are born into positions of wealth while other people are born into poverty. Many people are working to right this wrong. With the correct knowledge and tools, it's possible to eradicate hunger and make the world a more sustainable place.

CHAPTER FOUR

FOOD DESERTS

Many people, especially in low-income areas, live in food deserts. These are areas that don't have access to fresh food. According to the U.S. Department of Agriculture (USDA), a food desert exists in an urban area when there isn't fresh food within one mile (1.6 km). In a rural setting, a food desert exists when there isn't fresh food within 10 miles (16.1 km).

There are many reasons for food deserts, but perhaps the largest is wealth inequality. Many grocery store chains move to suburbs and neighborhoods with wealthier customers. Neighborhoods with food deserts often lack other necessities as well, including health services.

In Atlanta, Georgia, many poor people are affected by food deserts. A study by the Atlanta Regional Commission found that only half of low-income people have access to fresh food. In 2011 in Detroit, about 550,000 residents lived in food deserts. This contributed to Detroit becoming the world's number one consumer of potato chips.

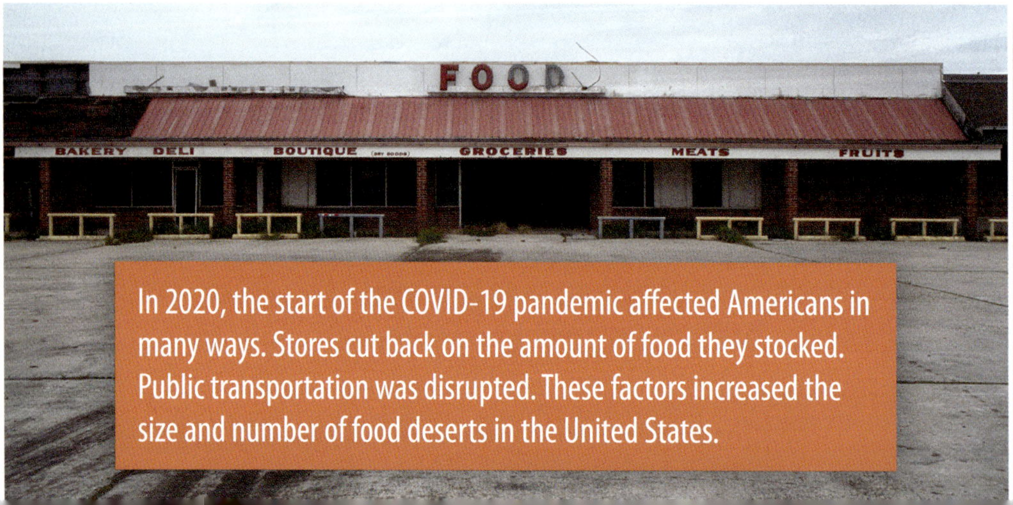

In 2020, the start of the COVID-19 pandemic affected Americans in many ways. Stores cut back on the amount of food they stocked. Public transportation was disrupted. These factors increased the size and number of food deserts in the United States.

Michelle Obama harvests vegetables with students. The Let's Move campaign stressed the importance of access to healthy foods.

In 2010, First Lady Michelle Obama focused on food deserts as part of the "Let's Move!" campaign. In 2014, the U.S. Congress set aside $125 million to build supermarkets in low-income neighborhoods. Some people believe that just building grocery stores doesn't really change a lot and that they don't solve the issues many people face. Many people don't have reliable transportation and it might not be safe to walk to the store. Ultimately, to fix food deserts, wealth must be distributed more evenly. Policy changes will be part of the solution to the problem of food deserts.

CHAPTER FIVE

FOOD'S ENVIRONMENTAL COST

All food has a cost. It takes resources to grow crops and raise animals. A farmer needs land, time, feed, fertilizer, and equipment. Still, growing certain types of food costs a lot more than others. This could be a financial cost, but there can also be an environmental cost.

It's sometimes useful to consider an ingredient based on its water intake. That's because fresh water is an important resource, but it's also limited. More than 97 percent of water on Earth is salt water, and many animals and plants need fresh water to live. Two-thirds of the average American's water footprint comes from food, and 80 percent of the water used in the United States is for agriculture.

Meat has a larger footprint than fruits, vegetables, and grains. That's because it takes a lot of grain and feed to raise animals. Raising cows, in particular, uses a lot of water. One pound of beef takes an average of 1,800 gallons (6,813.7 L) of water to produce. In comparison, it takes about 240 gallons (908.5 L) of water to produce a loaf of bread.

The chocolate industry makes about $50 billion a year. It's also a major contributor to deforestation, or the removal of trees and plants to make way for human development. The land that's needed to grow cacao beans, the main ingredient in chocolate, uses a lot of water as well: about 450 gallons (1,700 L) of water are needed to make everything that goes into a 3.5-ounce (100 g) bar of chocolate.

Deforestation so people can raise crops such as cacao is a huge problem. Deforestation not only affects the environment by destroying the habitats of many animals and plants, but it forces many people to live in poverty.

Unfair trade happens when the global market forces compromise at the expense of people. For example, market pressures may force a farmer to sell a product at a much lower price than it's worth. If they don't sell it at a lower price, they can't sell it at all. But when they sell at a lower price, they lose money.

The fair trade movement seeks to fix this. Next time you're at the store, look for a fair trade symbol on some packages. This is a circular mark with the word "fairtrade" beneath it. The movement uses that symbol to show that farmers and producers were paid reasonably for their work. The goal is for more small farms to remain in business.

But what kind of food is best for people and the planet? In early 2019, the World Wide Fund for Nature (WWF) UK partnered with a food company and released a list of 50 foods for the future. These foods make less of an impact on the environment.

One way to ensure that we protect people and the environment is to make sure the food we buy comes from sustainable sources.

Foods from the Future 50 List

- laver seaweed
- black beans
- lentils
- buckwheat
- quinoa
- okra
- spinach
- flax seeds
- walnuts
- alfalfa sprouts

ALFALFA SPROUTS

Lentils are extremely cheap and a great source of fiber and protein. They also have a very low carbon footprint—43 times smaller than beef.

CHAPTER SIX

THE STANDARD AMERICAN DIET

About three-quarters of the American population has a diet low in vegetables, fruits, dairy, and oils. In addition, many Americans eat way more sugar, fat, and salt than is recommended. In the United States, obesity and diabetes rates are among the highest in the world. According to the Centers for Disease Control and Prevention (CDC), more than 68 percent of all Americans are considered overweight or obese. One of the biggest reasons for this may be because portion sizes have gotten bigger. In addition, many Americans don't follow the food guidelines created by the U.S. Department of Agriculture and the U.S. Department of Health and Human Services (HHS).

In the United States, obesity rates are higher in low-income areas. One reason for this is may be that, for many people, the only food sold within walking distance is processed food found in corner stores or gas stations.

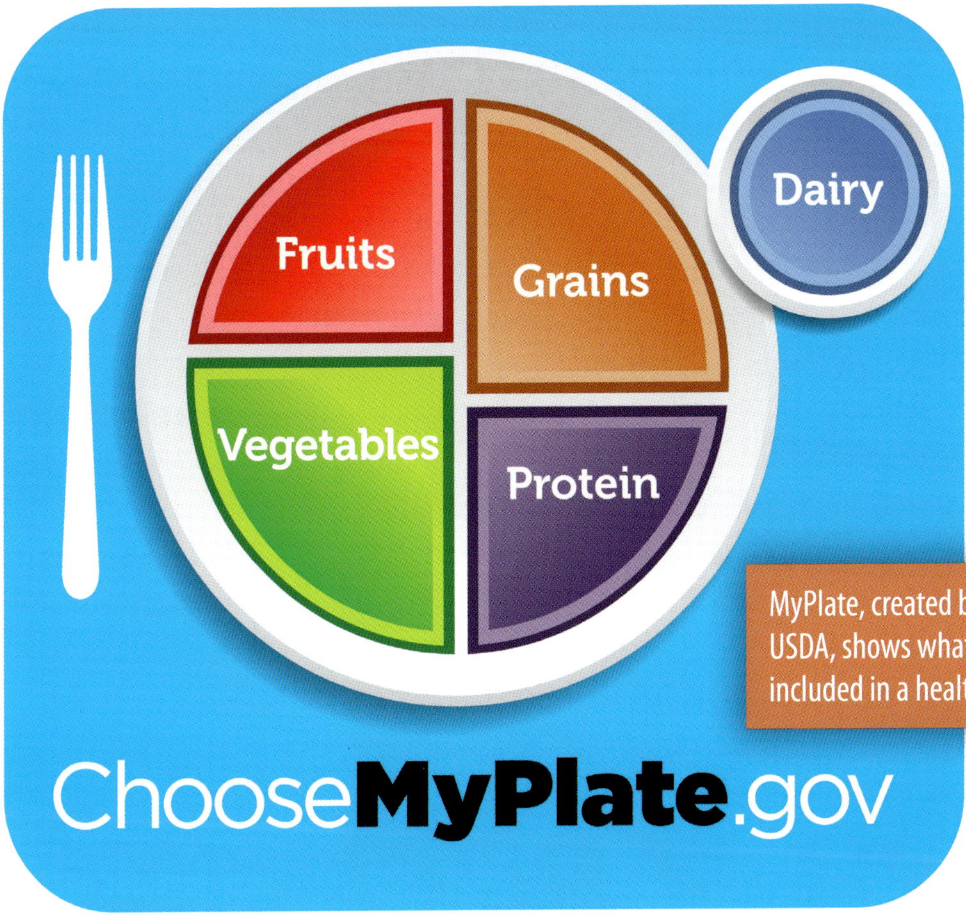

MyPlate, created by the USDA, shows what should be included in a healthy meal.

In recent years, the "westernized" diet—or the addition of more heavily processed foods and foods from fast-food chains—has spread to more places around the world. Globalization and how foods from the United States are produced and transported around the world have contributed to this change.

Nutrition and overall health are very closely linked: people who don't eat well tend to have more chronic health issues. Many scientists urge consumers to move away from heavily processed foods such as soda, packaged baked goods, instant soup, and instant noodles. Instead, for a healthier diet, people should eat more fresh fruits, vegetables, and nuts.

What we eat is the result of many factors, including what we've grown up with and what's marketed to us.

People in regions around the world eat differently based on what's available. On average, grain makes up 45 percent of peoples' daily calories. The healthiest diets are shown to be high in fruits, vegetables, and whole grains. In addition, diets that favor eating smaller portions have been proven to be healthier.

There are a few cultural diets that may promote health. One of these is the Mediterranean diet. The diet is high in whole grains, vegetables, and fruit. People around the Mediterranean also have cultural diets that include olive oil and nuts in moderation. The Okinawan diet is also known for its health benefits. People who follow the diet eat many vegetables and fruits, whole grains, and fish. One major vegetable in the diet is sweet potatoes, which are low in calories. The Nordic diet is also high in whole grains, fruits, vegetables, and seafood, which are native to Denmark, Finland, Iceland, Norway, and Sweden.

MEDITERRANEAN DIET

In some cultures, it's normal to have longer meals. Eating slowly helps people feel satisfied. It also helps them eat less.

As of 2018, France had the most sustainable food system in the world. In 2016, leaders introduced legislation that requires supermarkets to redistribute leftover food to charities and food banks. This was measured with the Food Sustainability Index, a global study on nutrition, sustainable agriculture, and food waste. Following France in ranking are the Netherlands, Canada, and Finland. The United States is ranked 26th on the index.

CHAPTER SEVEN

DIETARY CHOICES

One of the most important things we can do for the planet is to make small changes in our daily lives. You can find out where your food comes from!

When it comes to food, shopping local means the food doesn't have as much of an environmental impact. It doesn't have to travel long distances, and there's often less packaging. On average, produce from a grocery store travels about 1,500 miles (2,414 km) to get to your plate. Some food travels overseas on large shipping vessels. Other foods travel on airplanes. Usually food gets to the grocery store on trucks. Often, produce is picked before it's ripe so it can travel long distances without spoiling. It can also be refrigerated on its travels. Then, once it's reached its final destination, the produce may be sprayed with ethylene, a natural plant hormone, in order to cause it to ripen. There's a shorter shelf life for produce that's sourced locally, but eating meals with local ingredients often means you get the freshest food.

When you decide to spend money on local, sustainable produce, you're making a difference with your dollars. When you do that, you might help a local business stay around, and you put money back into your community. For every $100 spent at a local business, on average, $68 will stay in the community. That's because local businesses are more likely to buy products and services from other local businesses. In addition, when you shop local, you can be more informed about how your food is grown.

If your area has a farmer's market, you can shop there and get to know people in your community!

There are a lot of words thrown around when it comes to food, and there always seems to be a new fad diet. In 2018, the most popular diet in the United States was the ketogenic diet. This diet includes a very low-carb, high-fat intake. Other popular diets that year were the paleo diet, a diet that supposedly looks back to human diets of the Paleolithic era (including meats, seafood, vegetables, fruits, and nuts) and the Whole30 diet, a diet that supposedly removes foods that cause inflammation in the body. These diets aren't always healthy.

Vegetarian and vegan lifestyles are also gaining in popularity. Vegetarians don't generally eat meat products, but sometimes they eat eggs and dairy. Vegans generally don't eat any animal-derived products. Some people are even flexitarian, which means they usually follow a vegetarian diet with the option of adding meat to fit their lifestyles.

Think carefully about how you're nourishing your body.

Some people choose a diet that consists of organic foods. The term "organic" refers to the way farmers grow and process food. The USDA has a certification program for organic farms, and there are strict standards that must be met for a farm to be considered organic. These include methods that restrict synthetic fertilizers and pesticides and provide certain environments for livestock.

No matter what diet you choose to eat, it's important to make sure you're getting all the nutrients you need. Many people feel that certain diets, such as a vegan diet, are unhealthy. But if done correctly, these diets can be just as healthy as traditional diets.

CHAPTER EIGHT

FOOD ACTIVISM

From grassroots movements to big policy changes, many people are trying to change the food system for the better. However, what we choose to purchase and consume already has an impact. It dictates what the food industry will grow and provide. If something sells well, the market will change to accommodate it.

However, you can also work to change food policy. You can support politicians who insist on better regulations, including farm practices, food safety, and food labeling.

There's a lot one person can do. In 2014, *Time* magazine named three girls from Cork, Ireland, to a list of the influential teenagers of the year. The girls created a research project about bacteria that suck nitrogen from the atmosphere into the soil, which speeds up the germination of cereal crops. Among them was Sophie Healy-Thow, who's become further involved in agricultural practices. She's studied international development and food policy, given TED talks, and spoken at UN conferences about food insecurity. She's involved with an online social enterprise aimed at helping women in agriculture in developing countries.

Maureen Muketha is also fighting to make a difference with food. Muketha is from Kenya, where gender plays a big role in food production. In general, women do much of the planting and harvesting, but since men own the land, they often have the final say in where food goes. Muketha, who has a degree in nutrition studies, holds nutrition workshops where she teaches women about the benefits of a diverse diet.

The Royal Dublin Society named Emer Hickey, Sophie Healy-Thow, and Ciara Judge the BT Young Scientists of the Year.

CHAPTER NINE

FARMING METHODS OF THE FUTURE

While there are many people returning to traditional methods of farming, there are also many advancements being made in food production.

Vertical Farming

In this method, plants are grown on multiple levels, which means more plants can be grown in a limited indoor space. This method uses 95 percent less water than traditional farming. However, critics are concerned about the cost of putting this kind of system in place.

Robotics

Robots can address the issue of farm labor shortages. Robots are already doing the work of multiple farmers, including growing and picking and packaging. These robots can be programmed to pick weeds, so farmers don't need to spray their crops with herbicides. However, some people are worried that using robots will lower wages for people who rely on farms to make a living.

Plant-Based Alternatives

For meat lovers, the idea of going vegetarian or vegan can be scary. However, meat does have a high environmental impact. To this end, some companies have created new meat-free products that taste like meat without the high environmental impact. Some of these products have gotten so popular that food chains have begun serving them.

GMOs

Scientists can alter plants for better results in farming. They do this by inserting different DNA into plant cells. When that new plant grows and produces seeds, they contain the altered DNA. People are very divided on this technology. Some believe GMOs are necessary and helpful to feed a growing population, while others believe changing the DNA of food is dangerous.

A company called Impossible Foods makes the Impossible Burger, in part from soy. Its carbon footprint is 89 percent smaller than a burger made from real beef.

CHAPTER TEN

WHAT CAN YOU DO?

There's a lot you can do to change the food landscape in America and the world. You can let leaders know about the food-related policies that are important to you, and you can vote for politicians who promise to make changes.

For example, after many people voiced concerns about food safety, President Barack Obama signed the FDA Food Safety Modernization Act (FSMA) into law on January 4, 2011. The act shifts the focus from responding to foodborne illness to preventing it in the first place. To this end, food providers from farms to fast-food chains are required by law to handle food in a specific way. These laws have made food safer for many people.

Policy is incredibly important, but individual decisions are also crucial. Perhaps most important: start eating closer to home. Learn about where your food comes from and support the practices you feel are most beneficial.

Ways to Get Started

- Volunteer with a food kitchen.
- Throw out less food.
- Learn about where your food comes from.
- Write letters to politicians and government officials.
- Vote with your dollar: invest where it will do the most good.
- Plant a garden in your yard or in a community space.
- Organize a food drive.
- Learn to cook meals from scratch.
- Reduce your meat intake.
- Shop local whenever possible.
- Learn to compost food scraps to reduce waste.

About 1 in 6 people in the United States get sick from foodborne illness each year. The FSMA was put in place to make people safer.

Our diets change as people continue to learn new information about our food system and its impact on our health and on the world. It's likely that scientific discoveries will revolutionize our food system, and what we'll be eating in the future won't resemble what we eat today. For example, in 2015 a research team from Israel made a surprising discovery: that people's physical responses to the same food vary greatly. From this discovery, it's likely that we'll see more personalized diets in the future, maybe based on our very DNA. Another possibility is that we'll learn to tailor the food we eat so it will be more nutritious.

Still, there is a lot of room for growth, and that's where you come in. You have control over what you put into your body. There's a responsibility there too. It's important for each of us to be aware of how what we eat impacts the planet. We each need to make the right choices, personally and politically, so that the most good can be accomplished.

There are many people in the United States and across the world who don't have enough to eat. Food banks and soup kitchens need volunteers to collect and serve food to those in need.

We can eradicate hunger, and we can feed ourselves better. It starts with what we put on our plate. And that power is yours. What can you do today to help create a brighter future tomorrow?

GLOSSARY

accommodate (uh-KAH-muh-dayt) To make room for something or someone.

carbon footprint (KAR-bun FOOT-print) The amount of carbon dioxide emitted into the atmosphere by the activities of a person, company, or country.

chronic (KRAH-nik) Continuing or occurring again and again for a long time.

compost (KOM-post) To change plant material into compost, or decayed material used to improve soil.

diabetes (dy-uh-BEE-teez) A disease affecting the body's ability to produce or respond to the hormone insulin.

dictate (DIK-tayt) To command how something will be done.

distribution (dih-struh-BYU-shuhn) The way something is divided or spread out.

eradicate (ih-RAA-duh-kayt) To do away with completely.

germination (juhr-muh-NAY-shuhn) The act of germinating, or to cause to sprout or develop.

globalization (glow-buh-luh-ZAY-shuhn) The act or process of globalizing, or making something global.

hormone (HOR-mohn) A natural substance produced in the body that controls the way the body develops.

Industrial Revolution (in-DUH-stree-uhl reh-vuh-LOO-shuhn) An era of social and economic change marked by advances in technology and science.

inflammation (in-fluh-MAY-shuhn) A bodily response to injury or disease in which part of the body becomes warm, red, and swollen.

nutrient (NEW-tree-uhnt) Something taken in by a plant or animal that helps it grow and stay healthy.

obesity (oh-BEE-sih-tee) The condition of being significantly overweight.

pesticide (PEH-stuh-syd) A poison used to kill pests.

sustainable (suh-STAY-nuh-buhl) Able to last a long time.

synthetic (sin-THEH-tik) Something that is not made in nature.

INDEX

PRIMARY SOURCE LIST

Page 7
Upton Sinclair. Photograph. Ca. 1930s. Library of Congress.

Page 25
Emer Hickey, Sophie Healy-Thow, and Ciara Judge named BT Young Scientists of the Year. Photograph. Niall Carson. Dublin, Ireland. 2013. PA Images.

Page 29
President Barack Obama signs FSMA into law. Photograph. January 4, 2011. Pete Souza. Washington, D.C. 2011. White House photo.

WEBSITES

Due to the changing nature of Internet links, Rosen Publishing has developed an online list of websites related to the subject of this book. This site is updated regularly. Please use this link to access the list: www.powerkidslinks.com/SOGI/feeding